MOLLY

of

A Wartime
Childhood

Ray Moody

Rockumentarypress

Molly

Contents

Looking down Bean Street from Hessle Road

Copyright Notice

The photographic content contained within this book remains the copyright of the respective individual owner/s. Whilst every reasonable effort has been made to credit every photograph included in the book, because the majority of the photographs were taken around 80 years ago there may be some omissions of credits for which I apologise, and for which I will immediately rectify if contacted.

Fair Use Notice: The book may therefore contain copyrighted materials for which the use of has not been specially authorised by the copyright owner, I have made these available in order to record social history and specifically to advance understanding of what it was like to live in Hull, the most bombed provincial city during WW11. I therefore believe that this constitutes a fair use of any copyrighted materials. Photographs, artefacts, and information kindly provided by the Hull Daily Mail The Hull History Centre Carnegie Heritage Centre Hull

Chapter 1
12 POPLAR TERRACE

With its faded, maroon painted door, from the outside, 12 Poplar Terrace, Bean Street, looked like any other typical northern terraced house. One of six dwellings along one side of a flag-stoned yard, facing six on the other.

But inside, it was a singular house, a house full of its own odours and mysteries. The front passageway, as you entered, always smelling of damp linoleum. Passing by the door of the front room, a place that was seldom used, except at Christmas, when a fire would be lit in the grate. For the rest of the year, it would remain empty and only be pervaded by silence, with just the occasional sound of voices from the street penetrating its still air.

Beyond it, a door led into the small living room, where a window looked out onto a tiny backyard. The crammed room contained an ancient black Belgian stove, a horsehair settee, and a roughhewn wooden dining table. The table's cluttered surface was protected by an ancient piece of oil cloth. The clutter itself being hidden under sheets of ancient newspapers, the purpose of which was to catch the falling dust, which could be seen floating down in the rays of the morning sun.

Up a wooden flight of stairs, a back-bedroom served as the man of the house's carpentry workshop. It contained a woodworking bench, which was strewn with a whole range of seasoned work tools, leftovers from the man's seafaring days. In a corner of that room lay a small bed where the daughter of the house, Molly, would sleep.

Next door, the front bedroom contained the husband and wife's ancient brass bedstead.

Outside, at the rear of the premises the small backyard contained an ancient toilet, which, when flushed, sounded like the rush of a tumultuous waterfall. Next door to the toilet stood a coal shed in which there was a hutch containing rabbits. The narrow space on the inside of the slated roof of the coal shed also served as a place where rats would often nest.

The occupants of the house were a singular couple. The wife, Eleanor Land, had been born on 18 April 1898, and was one of four children. She had met her husband, Friedrich Raigrotzki, during the Great Depression of the late 1920s, as she had vainly attempted to sell brushes door to door. One of the doors she had knocked on was that of a German immigrant, a merchant seaman.

Friedrich Raigrotzki had been born on 21st March 1875 and lived with his father and mother and two sisters in the snowy provinces of East Prussia. In the winter, he'd had to ski to school. As a teenager his mother had been bitten by an Asp Viper whilst picking potatoes in a field and she had died. Soon afterwards, he had left home to sail the seven seas on both steam and sailing ships. Eventually he had booked a passage on a ship sailing from Hamburg to Grimsby. As a seaman, basing himself in England, he had signed on vessels sailing out of its many northern ports. including Whitby, Newcastle, Carlisle and Hull. Latterly, retired from the sea, he now relied on being selected by the foremen for casual labour on the Hull docks.

Often sailing into the port of Hull on the cargo ships of the Ellerman Wilson Line, he had met his first wife, Louise Van Borgaert. A Belgian lady, who was a few years older than Fred. She had run a boarding house for seamen down Waverley Street in Hull. and provided lodgings for foreign sailors coming into the port.

The couple had married in 1907. Sadly, after almost twenty years of their union, Louise had died of dropsy in 1926. She was buried in an unmarked grave in Hull's Spring Bank West cemetery, where Fred, many years later, would join her.

Two years after Louise's death, a 29-year-old Eleanor Land had knocked on Fred's door. Eleanor, or Leena, as she was known to her family, unlike her three sisters, had been put out to work at the age of 14. She had gone from menial job to menial job, cleaning the houses of the gentry. During the First World War, she had been sent away to Manchester to work in the bandage department of Smith and Nephew. At the end of the war, to thank her for her services, she had been awarded a gold-plated fob watch.

After the carnage of the First World War, there was a shortage of eligible young men for marriage and also occasionally being of a difficult nature, marriage had eluded her. To earn a living, she had continued to work in service, where followers were also frowned upon. Then one day she had knocked on Fred's door carrying a suitcase of brushes and they had struck up an acquaintance.

Fred down Poplat Terrace

7

Despite them appearing to be an odd couple. Thirty-year-old Leena was proposed to by the 54-year-old German immigrant, who had done so in his broken English, Leena had happily gone home and announced her forthcoming marriage to her father. Instead of congratulating her, when he had discovered that she was about to marry a German national, he had tried to strangle her. She had only saved by the timely intervention of Fred, who had been waiting outside the parental home, and who, with great difficulty, had managed to get her father's hands off Leena's throat.

Leena

Mr. Land's actions had been precipitated by the devastating First World War, which was still fresh in memory. Not that Frederich had seen action fighting the British in the trenches. Living in Hull with his first wife Louisa, on the outbreak of war, he had been interned by the British government at Knockaloe Camp on the Isle of Man. He was to spend three years there working in the camp kitchens. He was not to get released until 1919. A skilled carpenter, while in confinement at Knockaloe he had made Louise a trinket box, which had a picture of the camp painted on the lid.

The entrance to Knockaloe Camp, Isle of Man

The consequences of marrying Fred, meant that Leena was banned from her parent's house and wouldn't see her mother again for many years. It also meant that she took on her husband's nationality and had now become a German citizen.

After the marriage had gone ahead, their daughter, Molly had been born on the 2nd of July 1929. Fred adored her, and she adored her father and trailed him everywhere. At the age of three, she had followed him up some ladders in the backyard when he had been repairing the roof.

"Stand still!" he had ordered before rescuing her from falling to her death. Later, she had explained to him about the dog she had been playing with in the coal shed, which, when investigated, turned out to be a huge rat. Other adventures at that early age included sitting in the homemade coal cart for a trip down Bean Street whenever her father could afford a visit to the coal yard. These trips in the cart lasted long after Molly had started school.

With his native tongue being German, Fred spoke in broken English, often using the colloquial language he had picked up in England's Northern ports. Sometimes, to the amusement of Molly, and surprised neighbours, he would lapse into colloquial English, especially Newcastle slang, uttering such phrases as. 'Howay, man!' "Haddaway" or "Whey aye, man!"

Like the majority of other families living down Bean Street, the Raigrotzki's were poor. When a pair of Leena's bloomers developed too many holes and could no longer be darned, Leena would strategically wear another pair of worn-out bloomers on top to cover then up.

Some days, when Fred went to try to get casual labour down on the docks, he wouldn't be selected and would have to return home again. But despite the handicap of his German nationality, being seen as a good worker, he would often get work.

One day, whilst working on the docks, a sheet of rusty corrugated iron cut his finger and it turned septic. As it swelled up to almost the size of his arm, the finger had to be amputated. Taking himself down to the Hull infirmary in the city centre, a pad of chloroform was applied to his mouth while the surgeon hacked at his finger. Fred woke up several times during the operation, and the finger had to be roughly cut off. This resulted in a nerve in the finger becoming trapped, and in the future, whenever the end of that finger was touched, he would jump and let out a yell.

Whilst Fred spoke in broken English, Leena too used a wide range of quaint Hull expressions which Molly grew up listening to:

"You don't know 'A' from a bull's foot." She would say, meaning that Molly was too young to have knowledge of, or to understand something.

"Hush your mouth!" which she would say to Molly if thought that the neighbours were listening.

"She's got a mouth like dock gates has that one!" when referring to a person down the street who talked about the neighbours

"Don't play with her, she's lairy!" she would tell Molly when one of Molly's cheeky school friends had accompanied her home.

"It's onny lent!" Leena would tell Molly meaning that she wouldn't get away with something and retribution would come later.

"You're proper poo-noed!" meaning that Molly was silly for saying or believing something.

"It's all duck's quack is that!" suggesting that Molly or someone else was talking rubbish.

"Hark, they're bombing!" this would regularly repeat once the war had started and Hull was getting bombed. Leena often thought that she could hear the air raid sirens going off even when they weren't sounding.

"He's as well-known as bell-man is that one." Meaning that everybody should know who she was talking about.

"That I do know!" This is a phrase which Leena would often be repeated when Leena was determined about something.

"I'll tell mother!" This was also often said when Molly was being naughty.

"We'll be alright, once we get back on an even keel! Things would be okay once regular money was coming in again and the family could afford to pay their bills.

"She'd cut a currant in half would that one!" Meaning that someone was tight with their money.

And when Molly was crying, Leena would comment "Give over your gurning!" which she would tell Molly when she was sobbing and was naturally pulling a face.

Leena also never referred to people by their proper name, but by their characteristics. She often gave monikers to the people living down Bean Street. There was Dog Harry, Her at number two, the Bisto Kids, Cat Anna, that gadger from Simon's Terrace. Molly would often have to guess who she was talking about.

At the first sign of a cough, Molly would have a sheet of greaseproof paper, which had been warmed in the oven and liberally smeared with fat, sewn into her vest. As well as making her vests uncomfortable to wear, every time she moved, she would crackle. Like other mothers in those days Leena believed that by rubbing grease on the children's chests and vests, it would protect them from getting colds.

On a Monday in the Raigrotzki household it was washday. Leena, wearing a pair of tightly fitting wellingtons, would take a pram load of washing round the corner of Bean Street to the Regent Street washhouse. A large red brick building, it had skylights in its tin roof to let light in. The washhouse housed enormous sinks and washboards on which clothes would be vigorously scrubbed. There were also dolly tubs with podging sticks, coppers for boiling clothes, rolling machines for getting the water out of sheets. and drying rails which came out from the wall on a wheel.

The place was full of world-weary ladies. Amidst the heat, the noise, the steam and the soaking wet floor, Leena, like the other women, would do their weekly laundry. Then pushing the pram load of damp washing home, she would put it through her mangle. Unlike the other women down Bean Street, who would dry their washing on lines across the terrace, Leena hung hers in the small backyard and hoisted them on a clothes airer above the Belgium stove. Red faced, and dripping with perspiration on her return from the washhouse, she would often declare to Fred and Molly, "I've done a rully load of washing."

On returning home on one occasion, Leena discovered that the heat of the washhouse had welded hers already tightly fitting wellingtons to her legs. The rubber had adhered to her skin and all attempts to pull them off was in vain. The hot rubber had practically melted into to her flesh. Fred and Molly pushed and pulled at the wellingtons for hours, but in the end, there was no alternative but to cut them off.

This frequent carrying of 'rully loads' of washing to and from the Regent Street washroom, and the weekly tugging and heaving of the wet clothes, would later cause Leena to develop a prolapsed womb.

Regent Street Washhouse

Inside the Regent Street Washhouse

Like all of the other terraced houses down Bean Street, the property had no plumbed-in bath. Bath time in the house consisted of boiling a kettle to fill up the tin tub in front of the black leaded Belgian stove.

As Molly got older, there would also be occasional visits to the public slipper baths down Madeley Street. The baths were housed in individual cubicles and as you entered, the attendant would issue you with a thin slither of soap from a tin, the remains of which had to be handed in and returned to the tin on the way out. If the water cooled off while you were in there, you would have to shout to the attendant, "More hot water in number 3, please!"

The baths down Madeley Street

Fred rented an allotment down Institute Street, near Hawthorn Avenue on Hessle Road, which backed onto the Dairycoates railway line. He grew vegetables and the Riagrotski's would often enjoy a Sunday afternoon sitting cozily in the old potting shed drinking tea brewed on an ancient stove. Fred had worked hard over the years to turn a piece of what had practically been wasteland into a fertile garden. But just when it was at its peak, the Sunday trips to the allotment stopped when the owner of the land demanded his allotment back.

As a little girl, Fred kept rabbits in the coal shed and Molly would feed them. One Xmas she was presented with a pair of rabbit skin gloves and, to her horror, discovered that the rabbits in the backyard had disappeared.

In 1936, when Molly was five, the old king died and King George V1 was to be coronated. Each of the terraces down Bean Street, like many other streets across the country, set about planning coronation parties. Leena was asked to chip in towards food and drink for her child at the party, but being impervious to the ramifications that this might have, she declined.

On the day of the coronation, chairs and tables were brought out of the houses and put together down the terrace. Flags were hung from one side of it to the other. Walls were scrawled with the words, 'God save the King.' As the day went on, children from the street came and sat on the chairs and party hats were given out.

Molly looked on from the front room window of 12 Poplar Terrace and wondered why she hadn't been asked to join them. Gradually she worked her way onto the front doorstep of 12 Poplar Terrace and watched the children enjoying themselves in their party hats, as they ate from plates on the crowded table.

Above all the commotion of the children, Young Mrs. Hicks, a neighbour from down the terrace, noticed Molly and led her to the table. But then her sister, Old Mrs. Hicks, whose temperament wasn't as sweet as that of her younger sibling, had a word in her ear, "She hasn't paid!" she said, gesticulating towards the door of number 12.

"I'm so sorry!" young Mrs. Hick said as she led Molly back to her doorstep. But then she whispered in her ear, "Never mind, I'll bring you something later.

True to her word, when all the food had been eaten and the merry throng of children had left the table, Young Mrs. Hick came and collected Molly, and placed her on one of the now empty chairs. Molly looked on at the crumb littered plates, and the discarded tumblers, but she was still happy to be there. Then Young Mrs. Hicks brought her a large chocolate medallion wrapped in silver foil, and Molly beamed with gratitude.

While they made an odd couple, and her mother had some strange ways, Molly liked her parents. They were kind. Unlike most of the families down Bean Street, who often had as many as eight or more children, Molly was an only child. Many of the other fathers down the street were also quick to chastise their children, Fred wasn't like that, and Leena too hated to see children being given a 'leathering'.

In those early years, there would be occasional shopping trips down Hessle Road, to the Coop on the corner of Coltman Street for groceries. And at Xmas, visits to Woolworth, opposite the Langham Picture House. On a Saturday, the Raigrotzki's would also take a teatime stroll to a street market down Charles Street, when at that hour, any remaining meat would be sold off cheaply due to lack of refrigeration. Leena would also occasionally take Molly to see a show at the Alexandra Theatre down George Street, where they would sit in the Gods and Leena would tap her leg in time to the tunes coming from the stage.

On her birthday, Molly was taken down to Hull's marketplace to buy her a dog. Amongst all the stalls a man stood with a sack containing puppies. Molly reached into the sack to select one and grabbed the first one she came across. Fred wanted to check it out but Molly refused to be parted from it. She carried it all the way home and decided to call it Rover. A Yorkshire Terrier, as it grew it didn't anyone other than Molly touching it and would often give just one growl before biting someone if they continue to stroke it.

Coltman Street Coop

Approaching Sir Henry Cooper School from Anlaby Road

Suzanna's Terrace, Bean Street

Chapter 2

Bean Street

Bean Street was the longest residential street in Hull. It housed more people than any other thoroughfare in the city. At one end of it was Hessle Road, and at the other Anlaby Road. The street contained row after row of terraced houses, Temperance Terrace, Suzanne Terrace, Victoria Terrace, Simon's Terrace, William's Terrace, Wesley Terrace, Harriet's Terrace. The list was endless. When you walked down Bean Street, each terrace would be ticked off in turn. Poplar Terrace was situated almost halfway down the street.

When she was five, Molly started school. The official name for it was Sir Henry Cooper Board School, but, most local children called it Bean Street school. Molly's first teacher was Mrs. Pickering. A woman who Molly couldn't help noticing had an intriguingly, pockmarked nose.

Sir Henry Cooper School

Apart from being taught the three R's of reading, writing and arithmetic, Molly was also taught Needlework, but she could never gether stitches small enough to please the teacher.

On a Friday afternoon, the children were allowed into the classroom toy cupboard. Mrs. Pickering would issue the toys. Molly would always point to a dolly she liked, but was never allowed to play with it.

It was here in the infants that Molly met her first real friend, Selena Davis. Selena came from a family of eight and often had to look after her younger siblings. Molly liked visiting Selena's house, where her brothers would tease her. The Davis's kept a whole menagerie of animals, including chickens and rabbits.

Wellington Terrace

Playing out after school, they would often stand outside Mrs. Gorman's grocery shop on the corner of Harriet's Terrace and play I-Spy with the difference sweets in the window. One day Molly spotted a foil wrapped, cream fish in the window and saved up her pennies until she was able to buy it. The fish lived up to all of its expectations.

A young man with a huge head and deformed legs, would often be seen propelling himself up and down Bean Street in a homemade wooden cart. The man, was known locally as 'Arfa in a barra'. He looked menacing and would often beckon unsuspecting children over to him. Then, when they got close enough, he would attempt to hit their toes with a hammer. The man lived with his aged mother who was about half his size but she seemed to have full control of him.

On a Sunday Molly would go to Sunday School. The church was down an alleyway opposite Sir Henry Cooper School which led into Coltman Street. The preacher would stare down at her from his eagle headed lectern and Molly took in every word believing that he was talking directly to her.

The terraced houses of Bean Street backed onto Regent Street. The street had a children's playground which contained swings and a spider's web roundabout, and Molly and Selena would often play there. The ground beneath these rides was a wasteland of gravel, just waiting to cut some child's head or knee.

Regent Street Swings

They would also often walk down Anlaby Road to play in West Park or to borrow books from the Carnegie Branch Library. Molly was becoming an avid reader.

She also quickly learnt that there was a social division to Bean Street. Those at the Anlaby road end, known as the bottom of the street, considering themselves to be socially superior to those living closer to Hessle Road. Sometimes Molly would have to run an errand to a shop at the Anlaby Road end of the street, where standing on sentry duty at the entrance to De La Pole Terrace was a woman who would order her back. "You don't live down here, so get back!" she would say, "Get back where you live!" It was no good trying to explain that she needed to visit a nearby shop. "Go round!" she'd repeat, telling Molly to walk all the way back down Bean Street, turn onto Hessle Road and then walk down the length of Regent Street and along Anlaby Road before coming back down the end of Bean Street. When the woman was busy, she'd get her son, on leave from the army, to take over her duties. Standing to attention in his uniform, he was worse than his mother "Get back!", he'd snarl, as he stood there menacingly blocking the road. So, when she needed to visit that end of the street, Molly would have to make her way surreptitiously towards Anlaby Road hoping that her path wouldn't be blocked. If it was, she'd try to get as close as she could before attempting to run past the woman or her son. But even if she did get by, they would be waiting for her on the way back. Sadly, the son's sentry duties were later curtailed when he was killed during the war.

No way past the Bean Hotel

One day Molly had to visit a fish and chip shop at 7a Bean Street. In order to reach it, she would somehow have to get past the woman. When she was on her way there, and nearing the Anlaby road end of the street, a lady beckon to her from a nearby house. When Molly went over to see what she wanted the lady asked if she would bring her some fish and chips. Molly explained that she didn't mind running the errand, but said that she might not be able to get past the woman if she was waiting on the corner of her terrace. The kind lady said that she would keep watch, and if Molly was turned back, she would go and speak to the woman. On this occasion, the woman didn't come out of her house, so Molly was able to buy the fish and chips and earn a few pence for her efforts.

In those early years, some of the girls at school would occasionally make fun of Molly's surname. Molly Ri-hoss-tod, one girl would shout, and sometimes another girl would pull her hair and hit her and Molly would come home in tears.

"Hit them back, Molie!" her father would tell her in his broken English. Molly said that she daren't, but after she'd had her hair pulled once again, Fred showed her how to hit them. "Clench your fist and bring it down like a hammer on their nose."

It wasn't long before Molly was name called again and the girl reached towards her to pull her hair. But this time, as she did so, Molly drew back her arm, and like a hammer, hit the girl on the bridge of her nose with her closed fist. The girl's face went ashen and blood flowed freely from her nose as she ran off screaming. It had worked, and Molly gained confidence from this. There were other girls who would pick on her in the future, but the treatment advocated by her father was effective and the bullying soon stopped.

Several of the young men from the street would often drop in to have a chat with Fred. A ship's captain from his seafaring days, Captain Rawbottom, also occasionally looked in. But a regular visitor to 12 Poplar Terrace was Master Mariner, Captain Nicholl.

Fred had first served with him in 1898, signing on as a ship's carpenter onboard a steam ship. After that they had sailed on many more voyages together. Captain Nicholl considered that Fred could turn his hand to anything, so, when Fred needed a reference for employment, he would always be willing to write him one.

Whenever he called at their home, he always brought with him a present. One such gift was a China tea service.

When she was born, Fred had named Molly after Captain Nicholl's daughter Molly. Her middle name, Rita, had been chosen by Leena, who had named her after Rita Rosen, the daughter of a Hessle Road, shoe manufacturer who she had once cleaned for.

As well as being a skilled carpenter, Fred would experiment with a Cat Whisker radio set, picking up the BBC on a pair of headsets. He also told Molly that one day you would also be able to see pictures coming out of the radio.

Molly had never met her grandparents, but after not seeing her mother for several years, Leena discovered that her family had moved to a large bay windowed house down Jennings Street, off Cleveland Street in Hull. One day she tentatively turned up there with Molly, choosing a time when she knew that her father would be out at his work manning the railway crossing gates down Dansom Lane.

Dansom Lane Railway Crossing

So began a series of regular visits to her grandmother's house, where her adopted daughter, Nelly, would keep Molly in check. She would also meet her aunties, her auntie Doris who was very kind and a much sterner Auntie Ethel.

Molly liked the brass taps at her Grandma Land's house and during her visits, would often offer to polish them. Usually, she would be told that Nellie had already done it, but occasionally, when Nellie was out, Grandma Land would allow her to shine them.

On one occasion, when Grandma Land had moved to Alaska Street, off Holderness Road, Leena and Molly were late in leaving and they bumped into her father who had just finished work at the Dansom Lane railway crossing. Molly thought that there would trouble, as over the years, she had heard the story about him trying to strangle her mother and had built him up to being an ogre. But after acknowledging them, her grandfather simply said, "Have you been to see your mother?" It appears that he had an inclination that Leena had been visiting her and so the hostilities ended.

Daltrey Street

Harriet's Terrace

16 Gillott Avenue,
Anlaby Road
Hull.
13th June 1940

To who it may concern.

This is to certify that I have known Mr.
S Raignitski since 1898 when he served with
me as carpenter, on board a steamer and for
several years after. Of later years he has been
working on the Docks and doing jobs at his
own carpentering and joinering which is his
trade at which I must say he is a very
good hand especially at doing house repairs
etc. He is what you might call a real handy
man and can turn his hand to any odd
jobs

G A S Nicoll
Estered Master Mariner.

Barrage Balloon over Queens Gardens

Chapter 3

And then the Bombs Came

Months before the outbreak of war, Hull had already been preparing for possible conflict with Germany and had constructed communal air-raid shelters all around the city. Some, had been built along the edge of Queens Gardens At 3.20am on the morning of 4th September 1939, the first eerie air raid sirens sounded out over Hull. It proved to be a false alarm and the all clear was soon given.

A little while later when. Molly and her mother were shopping in the marketplace, the 'buzzers' went off again, Leena panicked and led her daughter down into the crypt of Holy Trinity Church, which had been designated as a communal air-raid shelter. Making their way down the ancient stone steps, the place was dark, damp and gloomy. As they sat there on a stone ledge, Molly wondered whether it was a safe place to seek shelter. If the church was bombed, the huge building would collapse down on top of them, trapping them in there. Luckily, the sirens were just a test and the 'All Clear' once again soon sounded. It wasn't until June 1940 that a bomb was actually dropped on the city.

Bomb damage to the church and the marketplace

Later on in the war, the market place and the area surrounding the church would suffer substantial bomb damage.

On the outbreak of hostilities, concrete and brick air-raid shelters were built down most of the terraces down Bean Street. Sand bags were piled up against them, and they often split. Air raid sirens were strategically placed around the city. One was placed on the top of the Priory Cinema at the end of Calvert Lane, An ARP warden, acting as a 'spotter' would stand next to it. Using a pair of binoculars, he would watch out for approaching enemy aircraft and be ready to activate the siren. The basement of Shell Mex House on the corner of Ferensway, as well as providing communal air raid shelters was established as Hull's main air raid command centre. From the outbreak of war in 1939, it housed the Air Raid Precautions Department, which was responsible for overseeing the protection of Hull and its residents. It was later devastated in the bombing and the command centre was moved to Queens Gardens.

A shelter was erected in the centre of Poplar Terrace. So, to not let any light out, an old rag was hung across its main entrance and it would flap in the wind. Fred seldom ventured into the shelter amongst the chattering women from the terrace. Not that they disliked him, "Are you alright Mr. Ri-hoss-key?" they would grin, unable to pronounce his name properly.

The air raid shelter down Poplar Terrace

Hull was to suffer its first daylight raid in June 1940 and the last attack on the city took place in March 1945. For the size of its population, Hull was to become the most bomb-damaged place in Britain during the Second World War. 86,715 of its houses would be destroyed or damaged. 120 of its communal shelters would be bombed. 250 domestic shelters would also be shelled.

There would be 82 air raids over the city and almost 1,200 people would lose their lives. A further 3,000 citizens would be badly injured. Many Hull families would be 'bombed out', some several times and they would have to look for another place to live.

Hull suffered so many air raids because as a port beside the river Humber it was easy to find. German aircraft would also fly over it to reach other targets such as Sheffield, Liverpool or Manchester.

Despite becoming the most bombed provincial city in Britain, Hull would never receive any recognition for its resilience and the suffering it endured during the constant bombing. It would also never feature in the newsreels like the raids on Coventry and London. This was because Hull was the subject of a 'D Notice' - a voluntary request for newspapers not to disclose certain information for reasons of national security. Churchill's wartime Cabinet was concerned that if it was known that Hull was suffering so many air raids it would lower morale. Therefore, the name Hull was banned from being mentioned in any of the radio and newspaper reports and the city was usually referred to as a 'North-East Coast Town'.

Between 1940 and 1945 Hull would spend more than 1,000 hours under air raid alerts. There would be 815 air-raid alerts and 152,000 citizens would be left homeless.

During one night alone, between the seventh and eighth of May 1941, more than 70 German planes dropped 110 tons of high explosives, and 9,648 incendiary bombs on the city. Some 420 people were killed, and another 350 were seriously injured.

By the time the war was over, only 6,000 of Hull's 91,000 houses were left undamaged. And while Hull's civilian war dead would officially be recorded as 1,243, recent research has shown that it is more likely to stand at 1,458, if you take into account those who died in accidents during the air raids, or committed suicide when their nerves couldn't take the bombing any longer.

With the war came the Blackout. No light was allowed to be seen coming from a house on an evening. And blackout curtains or material had to be fitted on all windows. Light bulbs were removed from street lights and cars had to have their headlights masked. To help to been seen in the dark, Molly, like other children, was issued with a luminous badge. The bottoms of lampposts were painted with white rings. Gas masks were also issued and Molly and Leena went and had theirs tested at a medical centre down Coltman, where Molly discovered that she could manipulate her mask to make a 'trumping' sound.

As the war went on, Leena became more and more frightened by the constant air-raids. So much so, that she would think that she could hear the sirens' eerie banshee wail, even when they weren't going off. But long before the air raids started, when Leena had heard thunder, she would go and sit in the gas cupboard underneath the stairs, but not before she had first gone through the ritual of first removing her false teeth.

As the war progressed, when the sirens went off, and Molly was slow to respond, Leena would give her one chance to come, and if she didn't do so immediately, Leena would dash off into the shelter without her.

In 1941, a public shelter down De La Pole terrace, towards the Anlaby Road end of Bean Street, was hit by a parachute mine and there were many deaths
. Fred would never go into the shelter, and he'd hang about the doorway of 12 Poplar Terrace, looking up at the droning planes in the sky as the searchlights based at the White City caught them in their beam and the heavy anti-aircraft gun battery at Costello playing fields opened fire.

On the eve of war, a Home Office pamphlet was published which stated that pets would not be allowed into public air-raid shelters. Many thousands of dogs and cats were needlessly destroyed during the first week of the war based on a false assumption that putting down the family pet was a patriotic and humane thing to do. The animals, it was claimed, on hearing the exploding bombs, were likely to go berserk and start running around the streets in demented, raging packs.

As dogs were banned, when Molly had once sneaked Rover in into the shelter, hidden in her cardigan, she had been forced to take him back into the house.

One evening when Molly was enjoying a nap on the settee the sirens sounded. "Are you coming!" Leena had said to Molly. But Molly felt sleepy and was comfortable on the settee so was reluctant to move. "Alright, then I'm leaving you!" Leena had said, and with that shot off into the shelter.

Fred had heard the siren, and, seeing Molly continuing to rest on the settee, managed to persuade her to follow her mother out into the shelter. No sooner had she entered it than there was a huge explosion, which blasted the whole terrace. Most of the house windows were blown out, including the front room window of 12 Poplar Terrace. So loud was the blast that Fred had left his normal position on the doorstep and dived into the relative safety of the entrance of the shelter. When the all-clear siren sounded and Fred, Leena and Molly returned to their house. They found the front room window frame hanging out and the glass from it scattered everywhere.

On entering the living room, they discovered that the settee on which Molly had recently been laying was showered in glass. The pillow on which she had been resting her head had a huge dagger of glass stuck through it. The room was also filled with black soot from the chimney. It was spread over everything, including the kitchen table. Molly began anxiously shouting for Rover, and what appeared to be a huge black rat suddenly emerged from beneath the Belgian stove. It was Rover, and he was totally covered in soot.

The house windows were repaired by the local authorities, and the settee had to be thrown away. But an attempt to claim for it was thwarted because they had not kept the evidence.

One day towards the end of the war, when the siren had sounded, Molly and Leena were sitting in the shelter with the rest of their neighbours when they suddenly heard what appeared to be the sound of a motorcycle engine. "Who could possibly be out on a motorcycle in this?" exclaimed Leena. But Molly had recently read about the 'flying bombs' the V1 and the V2 rockets. The sound of the motorcycle got closer and closer, then suddenly the engine cut out. Molly knew that this meant that the bomb had run out of fuel and would now float to the ground. Bracing herself for the blast, there was 10 or 20 seconds of silence, and then suddenly a huge explosion at the bottom of the terrace. The bomb had dropped on Binningtons' Lemonade factory, which stood in Regent Street, just over the wall from the terrace.

Several houses down Poplar Terrace were also bombed out and became unoccupied. The last house at the end of the terrace had also caught the blast, blowing out a wall and all of the doors and windows. After this the derelict house provided a quick passageway into Regent Street.

Lord Haw-Haw, who broadcast Nazi propaganda to the UK from Germany during the war, actually came on the radio and mentioned Binnington's and the raid, claiming that the factory was making armaments. Molly and Selena visited the derelict premises later and found thousands of small metal parts scattered about the place.

Bean Street suffered several direct hits during the war, the worse one being at the Anlaby Road end of the street, when De La Pole Terrace was totally annihilated. One family, a grandmother and granddaughter, who lived down there, had changed their shelter that night and had escaped the bombing. But a few weeks later, when the buzzers had gone off again, they'd had sought shelter down La Trobe Terrace in Regent Street. The shelter suffered a direct hit and both the grandmother and granddaughter, were killed.

Bean Street School experienced bomb damage twice during the war and for several months the children had to be removed to Thomas Barton Holmes school down South Parade.

Later on in the conflict, Fred managed to get paid work on a freelance basis from the estate agents, Larards. He repaired their housing stock's bomb-damaged window frames and replaced broken sash cords. But Larards were slow to pay him, and often quibbled about how much work he had done, so he eventually gave it up. He also got accepted by the Civil Defence as a Fire Watcher and was based on the roof of Atkinson and Prickett down the Land of Green Ginger. Because of his German background, it initially took some convincing that Fred would actually put any fires out and not accelerate them.

Molly and Selena would often set up home in many of the bomb-damaged houses, sitting in the discarded armchairs and pretending to be keeping house.

On the 6th August 1941, King George and Queen Elizabeth came to the city to see firsthand the damage that Hull and its people had endured. Hordes of people lined the city centre and spread all the way along Hessle Road. Cheering crowds greeted the entourage as they passed by. Winston Churchill also visited the city and joined members of the ARP as they searched the rubble of Bean Street for survivors.

The Home Guard in Queen Victoria Square

Florence Atkinson: Age 14yr.   7.2.42.

"What happened to me and what I did
          in the Air-Raid."

I was very frightened when we had a
big blitz in all kinds *various* of districts of Hull
There was one big blitz on the —
and Thursday night, and we were *were* very
frightened indeed, for we live in Bean
St., and We heard a very loud
long whistle and it *was it* which
fell in Regent St. I was in the
house at the moment, *seated* under the
table, and all the fire flew out of
the grate and burnt my legs. We all

μW

Mary   Age 12 years   9.2.42
            What Happened to me and
                  what I did in the Air Raids
It was Friday July the sixth *1940* and it was
a stormy day to It was five-o-clock and
we were having our tea when the buzzars
went; then just I after *they* it finished we heard
a bomb dropping and then a loud clap
of thunder. My father said, "You had better
go across to the shelter, It look's bad".
      Every body was *in a* panic, running about
the street, when a little boy cried out,
"There's something on fire up in the sky". All
eyes gazed up to the sky. I thought, "I
wish Old Hitler was on fire". It was a
barage balloon *barrage balloon* which had caught fire and
soon a lot more caught *fire*. The Nazis could
not resist dropping I the rest of *his* the load
but *and* he was soon caught by our brave lads.
      Then the "All-clear" went and I thought
"The more you come to bomb us the more

37

Hammonds Department store, before and after the bombing

Bomb damage down Chapel Street, close to the Pioneer snack bar

Bomb blast has smashed all of the windows down Midland Street

The Bombing of Prudential Building near the City Hall, 7th May 1941

The Cecil Cinema prior to it being bombed

The Alexandra Theatre, George Street

Bombed in 1941, ruins of Alexandra Theatre

Villa Place

Porter Street

The Shell Mex Building, Headquarters of the Air raid command centre

Enemy aircraft spotting on the top of Hull Guildhall

The Playhouse Cinema, Porter Street, before it was bombed

LUFTWAFFE CONCENTRATE
IN HEAVY RAID ON HULL

MANY CASUALTIES FEARED

Widespread Damage: Ring of Fires

R.A.F. START MOI RHINELAND FIRE

The wartime terraces of Bean Street

Bean Street Mission Hall

The bottom of Alexandra Terrace

The top of Alexandra Terrace

Midgley Terrace

Bottom of Midgley Terrace

Victoria Terrace

Richmond Terrace

Harriet's Terrace

Franklin Terrace

Bottom of Poplar Terrace

Bottom of Industrial Terrace

Bottom of Franklin Terrace

Wesley Terrace

Alexandra Terrace

Victoria Terrace

Marrs Terrace

Wellington Terrace

Chapter 4

Miss Treff

When Bean Street School was bombed, the children were transferred to Thomas Barton Holmes School on South Parade, off Anlaby road. Known as T. B. Holmes school, it too was bombed and eventually, Bean Street school was repaired, and the children were able to return.

When she was eleven, Molly went up into the senior part of the school. Her new teacher was Miss Treff who had been transferred there from T B Holmes school. She was to become Molly's nemesis.

On the afternoon of the first week with her new teacher, as Molly entered the classroom, she asked a friend what the lesson was. Her friend replied, painting. "Oh, good I like painting! "Molly had responded. Miss Treff heard her, "Stand in that corner and face the wall!" she roared.

Molly obediently went and stood in the corner of the classroom and spent the whole lesson there. The following week when it was the painting lesson again Miss Treff found some other excuse for having Molly once again go and spend the lesson standing in the corner of the classroom. This also happened again the third week. On the fourth week, Molly automatically went and stood in the corner of the classroom. When Miss Treff noticed her standing there, she asked her what she was doing. Molly told her. "I've stood here for the past four weeks, so I'll stand here for the rest of the term, and she did.

Molly noticed that Miss Treff also regularly picked on another girl. The girl was from a really poor family and they couldn't afford an alarm clock, and so she was always late for school. Telling her off for arriving late, Miss Treff would pull the poor girl about like a rag doll.

Not that Molly didn't have allies. With her always being top of the class and working hard to stay there, she was thought well of by the Head Teacher. So, when later, the Head was looking for a girl to be captain of the school, she spoke with Miss Treff, who suggested Joan Taylor. "No, I think Molly," the head had replied, which was much to Miss Treff's chagrin. Molly also became head of Red House the school Swimming Secretary. Accompanying the children to the Madeley Street Swimming Baths, each week, she took notes and fed back on performances and activities in the school's morning assemblies.

She did, however, nearly lose her captaincy. One day when was with another girl in the school store cupboard tidying things up, they both wondered what a pile of clothes were doing high up on a shelf. Inquisitive, Molly clambered up to take a look and discovered that they were baby clothes which had been especially made by the Needlework teacher and her classes. The clothes were to be given to the needy. But as he jumped back down in her kilt, she accidentally knocked over a bottle of ink which spilt all over the clothes.

Molly was in tears and beside herself. On telling Miss Treff, about the accident, she immediately told the head, who asked Molly why she was up there. In between her tears Molly had explained that it was pure inquisitiveness. The clothes had to be washed and for a week it was considered whether Molly should be relieved of her captaincy, but in the end, the Head thought that she had suffered enough.

Miss Treff would often sit on a desk top while she taught the class and Molly would giggle at the sight of her elasticated, pink bloomer legs which showed just above her knees. She also had a red face and blue veins on the end of her nose. When she angry with a class member she would get her face close to the offending pupil. When Molly was the object of her wrath, and Miss Treff came close to her, she couldn't help but look at the protruding veins on her nose and had to stifle her laughter. Miss Treff would tell her to, "Take that smile off your face, or I'll knock it off.

As the war dragged on, Miss Treff decided to have a class charity box to collect money for the war effort. This was stood on a front row desk belonging to one of the school girls. The money collected in the box was added up every week and sent off. One week Molly asked her father for a three-penny bit for the collection. Giving her it, she duly went to school and placed it in the box. At the end of the week, the box was opened in full view of the class to see how much money had been collected. Craning her neck, Molly could see that her father's hard earned golden three-penny bit wasn't there. The box only contained pennies and half-pennies. Upset about it, Molly put her hand up and told Miss Treff that she had put a three-penny bit in the box and it wasn't amongst the collection. It looked as though the girl on whose desk it was on had taken it out. Miss Treff said that Molly must have been mistaken, but the box was the following week moved to Miss Treff's desk.

Every morning the children would assemble for morning prayers in the main school hall. One morning, as prayers were about to be said, Molly was accused by Miss Treff of talking and not taking the occasion seriously. She was called out and made to go to the front of the massed children. She was then told to kneel down in front of them, and while the rest of the children stood, she knelt on her knees to say her prayers.

That lunchtime, on her way home from school, Selena Davis went and told Leena that Molly had been made to kneel to pray. Wearing her washday wellingtons and sporting a red face from the heat in the washhouse, Leena marched down to the school to ask why. Miss Treff, brushed it off, saying that it had been a privilege for Molly to kneel to say her prayers and she said that if there was enough room, then everyone would kneel. "That's as may be," replied Leena, "But I don't want her kneeling again!"

When the war started and the sirens went off during the school day, the children would have to file out into brick air raid shelters which formed part of the school walls. To keep moral up, Miss Treff would ask the various members of the class to sing or recite something. One girl would do a George Formby impression, and would have everyone in stitches. Miss Treff would often ask Molly to recite, 'You are old Father William' from Lewis Carroll's Alice in Wonderland.

"You are old, father William," the young man said,
and your hair has become very white;
And yet you incessantly stand on your head --
Do you think, at your age, it is right?"

There were also some occasions when the class would be allowed to come to school wearing fancy dress. Molly had been given a flouncy Snow-White costume by Captain Nicholls' daughter, who ran a dance school down Albert Avenue and she would often wear it. One girl, Annie Woodward, would come dressed as a chimney sweep, with a blackened face and a fag end stuck in her mouth. She always won a prize.

A Bean Street Terrace

The bombing of Bean Street

Churchill amidst the ruins of Bean Street

After the bombing, Bean Street, looking through to Coltman Street

Bomb damaged Regent Street

After a raid, T. B. Holmes School, South Parade

Bombed out Thomas Barton Holmes School

La Trobe Terrace, Regent Street

Bombed out terrace Regent Street

Chapter 5

The Dentist

One day at school, there was a visit by the dentist to inspect the children's teeth. All of the girls lined up to take it in turns to have their mouth checked. Molly loved sweets and sure enough, on her teeth being examined, the dentist handed her a card to take home to her mother. It advised that Molly had tooth decay and should see a dentist. The names of all the children receiving a card were written in on the blackboard by Miss Treff.

Molly gave the card to her mother and a few days later Leena took her down Coltman Street to visit a dentist. The dentist looked into Molly's mouth and advised that she needed some extractions. With that he then reached for a pair of pinchers.

"What are you doing?" cried Leena.
"I'm going to take them out?
"Without an anesthetic?"
"There're only milk teeth, they'll soon come out."
Leena whisked Molly out of the chair.

Outside the building, perturbed, Leena spoke to two passing women and told them about how the dentist was going to take Molly's teeth out without an anesthetic and now she didn't know where to go. The women advised her to try the children's hospital down Park Street.

A few days later, Molly stood in a corridor along with a line of other children waiting to see the hospital dentist. A door at the end of the corridor would sporadically open and a child would disappear through it. The queue of children began to gradually get smaller and eventually Molly had made her way to the front. The door then opened and Molly was greeted by a sea of faces standing around a large black chair. A woman closed the door then said, "You're Molly, the nervous little girl?" Molly nodded her head. The next minute she was grabbed from behind and thrown into the chair. The next minute the woman had sat on her knees, her head was thrust back and a black rubber mask covered her nose and mouth. As the gas seeped through the mask, Molly was unable to breath, and a sound like thunder filled her ears. Eventually, she blacked out.

The next thing she knew was the back of her dress being ripped as she was thrown with her bare back onto a cold rubber sheet to bring her back to consciousness.

Whenever the dentist visited the school in the future, Molly would quake as she was handed the dreaded card. The whole procedure would then begin again with and the names of those with 'dirty mouths' being written on the blackboard by Miss Treff. Molly would take the card home and hide it underneath the cloth on the table. The names of those requiring dental treatment would slowly be removed from the blackboard, until finally, there would only be Molly's name and that of another poor girl left. And Miss Treff would draw the children's attention to the fact that there were now only two people in the class with dirty mouths. And Molly would finally have to show the card to Leena who would explain to her that if she left the decaying tooth, then it would turn the one next to it bad. And so, the whole nightmare of a visit to the dentist and the dreaded black rubber mask would continue.

Park Street and the way to the Children's hospital

Chapter 6

Stitches

One day, soon after she was eleven, during playtime at Sir Henry Cooper School, Molly and her classmates decided to play a game of tig. They all joined hands together and formed a circle, leaving one girl in the middle as the tigger. The girls all swayed this way and that in an effort to avoid getting tagged. Suddenly the school bell went and the two girls on either side of Molly immediately let go of her hands. Caught off balance, she fell backwards, hitting her head on a stone seat in the playground. While the blow hurt, Molly picked herself up and followed the rest of the girls into school. Then one of the girls walking behind her said, "There's blood on your collar!" "I know there is!" replied Molly, believing it to be a joke. But then she touched the back of her head and her hand come away covered in blood. Molly let out a scream that could be heard across the playground. A teacher came over and ushered Molly into the school washroom, where an older member of staff was busy washing paint pallets. On seeing the blood seeping down Molly's head, the woman immediately began dabbing the wound with the same dirty cloth she had been washing the paint pallets with.

Meanwhile, Selena, having heard Molly's scream and realizing that she had split her head open, rushed out of school gats down to 12 Poplar Terrace, where, after hammering on the door, made Leena aware of Molly's plight. Leena, who was still wearing her washhouse wellingtons, then dashed behind Selena, following her back to the school.

She arrived there just in time to see the classroom assistant still using the dirty paint rag to try to stem the blood flowing from Molly's wound. Leena quickly snatched the cloth away from her head, and realizing that the wound needed attention, set off with Molly to seek medical help. Speaking to some passing women they suggested that she took Molly to a Medical facility which had been opened up down Regent Street for the duration of the war. On entering the place, Leena was told that the establishment only dealt with gas victims and was advised to take Molly to the children's hospital down Park Street.

Arriving at the hospital, a distraught Molly was dealt with immediately. The wound would require stitches. Lying her face down, while a policeman held the sides of the wound together, a nurse, without the use of an anesthetic, quickly attempted to stitch it. Meanwhile, Molly hysterically bore it all.

After her ordeal, Leena and Molly walked back home to Bean Street. Sitting in an old armchair, as the stitches tightened amidst the dried blood, Molly became frightened to move her head in case she snapped her stitches. For two days she sat there, barely daring to move. But the moment she did, she heard a ping and blood seeped down her face denoting that the stitches had burst. Leena quickly got her coat on, and took a near hysterical Molly back to the hospital where the stitches had to be reapplied.

Molly once again returned home and sat there, barely daring to move, lest a stitch should break. Several more days passed and her wound started itching. Molly asked her mother to take a look. Lifting the pad covering the wound, Leena quickly put it back down again. Then, a couple of minutes later, slyly suggested, "I think we might just pop back to the hospital, they might have something to help with the itching.

Arriving at the Children's Hospital down Park Street, Leena told Molly to wait for her at the bottom of a stairwell while she went and had a word with the doctor. A few moments later a nurse appeared, "You're the little girl who'll be staying with us for a while.
"No!" replied Molly, believing that the nurse had made a mistake. "You're Molly aren't you, you've a poorly head and it needs looking after." Shouting for her mother she was nowhere to be seen and Molly thought she was being kidnapped.

Apparently, the cut had turned septic, and needed hospital care. The nurse led Molly away to a ward which was full of babies and was told to get into a bed. Later that day, like the babies, she was given bread and milk to eat.

Molly sat in the bed believing that some terrible mistake must have been made and that her mother would appear at any moment.

But as night fell, the air raid sirens went off over Hull and as bombs crashed down on the city the nurses and porters ran into the ward to collect Molly and the babies. They were taken down into the basement of the hospital, where Molly was given a baby to look after.

That evening the bombing over Hull was so intense that the next day it was decided to evacuate all of the children to a stately home out in the East Riding which was being used as a hospital. Molly and the rest of the children were put into ambulances and driven out into the countryside. Having a vivid imagination, she thought that the Germans must have landed and would never see her mother and father again.

Molly spent weeks recuperating, with one nurse telling her that if her head didn't get better, it would have to be replaced with a turnip. The hospital was a strange place. The lady of the manor would occasionally come round to inspect the children. Molly continued to receive the same small amount of bread and milk that was being given to the babies and when she visited the toilets, handfuls of horsehair had to be used instead of toilet paper.

Having not seen her parents for over a month, each day the doctors visited her on his daily rounds Molly would beg him to let her go home. After inspecting her head, "You're not better yet!" he would say.

On an evening, when one of Molly's favourite nurses was on night duty, Molly would sneak out of her bed down the ward to sit with her at her desk. The ward was full of babies and the nurse would encourage Molly to go and comfort them if one started crying.

Despite enjoying her nightly sojourns to look after the babies and the friendship of the nurse, Molly continued to implore the doctor to allow her to go home. She wondered what had become of her parents. Were they still alive, had the Germans got them, had their house been bombed and they had died? As time went on, the doctor could see that Molly was clearly becoming affected by not being able to see her mother and father and eventually, because of her daily beseeching considered that Molly might not ever recover fully unless she returned home, so the doctor finally gave way.

After her initial joy at being able to go home, Molly began to feel guilty about leaving her favourite nurse and the babies behind. So that when Leena made the long journey to collect her, Molly appeared distant. She hadn't seen her mother for months and meeting her again she felt like a stranger.

Back home, Molly continued to feel strange after the routine of the hospital and her mother began to think that she was losing her. It was only when Leena began crying with the unresponsiveness being shown by her daughter, that Molly finally came around and felt joyed at last to be home.

Her return was celebrated by a party with a large selection of food being provided by Captain Nicholl. Despite it being wartime, there was tinned salmon, biscuits and a jelly. Leena also baked one of her thick crusted apple pies.

A jolly outing from the Engineers Arms, Bean Street

Chapter 7

INTERNMENT

On the outbreak of the Second World War, Winston Churchill was asked what should be done about all of the foreign nationals living in Britain. His reply was brief, "Collar the lot!" This was to be Britain's policy of internment during the Second World War. Foreign nationals, were to be classed as enemy aliens.

It wasn't long after the war started that a letter arrived for Fred. It explained that he was classified as an enemy alien and as such had to report to Paragon Railway Station in Hull for transit to Strensall Army Barracks in York. From where he would be transported to Liverpool and then shipped over to the Isle of Man.

Fred wasn't a stranger to the place, as he had spent three years of his life at the island's Knockaloe Camp, near Peel on the Isle of Man, during the First World War.

Fred hadn't been the first 'foreigner' down Bean Street to be sent for. An Italian neighbour living with his family just around the corner from Poplar Terrace had already been collected.

When Leena had seen the letter, she had been very cross.
"This is all your fault for not getting naturalised!" she had admonished Fred.

What Leena hadn't also realised was that when she had married Fred, she too had taken on his nationality, and now, for all intents and purposes, she too had become classified as a German citizen.

When Fred left home for his internment, so too had the little enough income he brought in. With no money to feed Molly, Leena, who had for many years been a regular customer at a local grocery store down Bean Street, visited the place and explained to the owner her plight. After telling the shopkeeper about her predicament with Fred being interned, she asked for a few items on tick, until she could sort things out. Despite having shopped there for many years, nothing was forthcoming.

Leena then applied to the National Assistance Board, but her now German status weighed heavily against her. When she finally managed to convince the panel that she and her daughter were destitute, they made a visit to 12 Poplar Terrance to carry out a means test. Seeing that Leena was wearing a gold wedding ring, they advised that it could be pawned and also that there was no need for the living room table, it too could be sold.

Leena duly pawned her wedding ring and was eventually awarded a few shillings in vouchers by the Assistance Board. These could only be used to purchase very basic items of food such as bread. Leena then set about looking for casual employment, taking on menial domestic cleaning jobs that kept her out all day. She also took work washing the blankets of TB patients at the former Anlaby Road workhouse which had become the Western General Hospital.

Meanwhile, after arriving at Douglas pier on the Isle of Man, Fred discovered that his previous home at Knockaloe camp, near Peel, had been demolished. He was instead to be accommodated in one of the many boarding houses on the seafront at Douglas. The houses had been sectioned off behind barbed wire and were guarded by armed soldiers. Each of the properties housed a number of internees and each of them was given a job to do. Fred was made the house cook.

Fred had been lucky. The Italian man from around the corner of Poplar Terrace, Mr.Forti, had also been taken like Fred to Liverpool. But instead of him being sent off to the Isle of Man, he discovered that he was being deported by ship to an internment camp in Canada. The ship was called the Arandora Star and its role was to transport Italian and German prisoners to camps overseas. All of the internees onboard the Blue Star Line's former passenger ship came from a temporary internment camp based at Warth Mills in Bury. Sadly, forty miles out from the coast of Ireland, the Arandora Star was torpedoed by a German submarine and Mr. Forti and 804 others, including a Mr. Pacitto, a Mr Pratti and a Mr. Ferri, also Italian residents from Hull, lost their lives. Bodies from the ship were washing up on the Irish coastline for many weeks.

Fred was faring better this time on the Isle of Man. Living in one of the seafront boarding houses that people would have paid to have had their holidays in prior to the war. While all of his fellow internees carried out their allocated jobs with the house, he was the house cook and never went hungry.

Although, letters were censored, Fred was allowed to write home to Molly and Leena. In them, he always wrote that he was worried they weren't getting enough food and felt guilty that he had plenty on the Isle of Man. His letters were written using his limited command of English and he wrote the way he spoke. The letters would always begin, with the words "Dear Wif and Dortor".

In 1940, when Fred had been in the camp for just over a year, a Member of Parliament, chanced to be canvassing votes, down Bean Street. On opening her door to him, Leena was asked whether he could count on her vote during the forthcoming general election. "I'm voting for nobody!" Leena had told him. The canvasser, was Walter Windsor, the standing MP for Central Hull. He then asked Leena why she wouldn't be voting.

She explained how her German husband had been interned on the Isle of Man, which had left her with no income to pay the rent or feed her daughter. Clearly showing concern, he took notes and said that he would raise the issue in the House of Commons. Thanks to his intervention, Fred was released from internment in 1941 and was able to return home.

It was later decided that due to the war, there would not be an election in 1940 and the next one would take place at the end of hostilities. A strange coincidence, is that Walter Windsor, who had been the standing Member of Parliament for Hull Central since 1935, was to later prepare for the 1945 election, by setting up offices in a room at the Broadway Hotel, in Hull.

By then Molly had left school and had got a job there as the hotel's receptionist. One day, a chambermaid, found Walter Windsor dead at his desk when she had entered his room to clean it.

Fred, far right at Knockaloe Camp, Isle of Man

Prisoners gardening at Knockaloe Camp, Isle of Man with the prisoners huts in the background

The Comparative luxury of the seafront houses at Douglas, IOM

Bridgegate, Howden

The Market Place, Howden

Chapter 8

Evacuation

On reaching the age of eleven Molly had entered the senior part of her school, Molly's first teacher in the seniors was Miss Poole. With the coming war, Miss Poole began planning to evacuate to Canada. During a conversation in the schoolyard between Leena, Molly and her teacher, Miss Poole offered to take Molly with her. When Leena was asked whether she might consent to this, Leena, instead of immediately saying no, replied, "It's up to Molly!" Molly, was quite perturbed by the thought of leaving her parents and had heard that even passenger ships were regularly being torpedoed by German submarines as they crossed the Atlantic. So, she firmly said no.

On the outbreak of war, the government knew that the major cities of Britain would be bombed. So, they decided to move children to safety in the countryside. Young children (under five) were allowed to take their mothers with them, but older children had to go on their own.

Every day, children would arrive at school with their small suitcases packed just in case when they got there, they were told that they were going to be evacuated. It was kept a secret until then.

In Hull, school children were marched down to Paragon railway station where they boarded mystery trains to their new homes.

The war had been raging and the bombs had been dropping on Hull for a while when it finally became too much for Leena. So it was decided that she and Molly should evacuate to the countryside leaving Fred behind to look after the house. Leena had borne the constant bombing by taking her false teeth out and plugging up her ears.

Day by day children had gradually been disappearing from Molly's school as they had been evacuated. Normally, the children would be put on a train with a teacher and transported to some village where they would be selected and taken into a family. Leena had no thought of leaving her daughter alone with strangers. She would evacuate with her.

Hearing on the grapevine that an evacuation train had been arranged to leave from Paragon Station, the following day, Leena and Molly presented themselves at Sir Henry Cooper School, where they met the rest of the evacuees and the teachers accompanying them. From there the party trooped down Anlaby Road to the railway station where they were directed to board a waiting train.

Every carriage was soon crammed full of evacuees. There was no indication anywhere of the train's destination. But local knowledge had it that Hull children had already been evacuated to places such as Scarborough, Filey, Malton and various villages throughout the East Riding.

When a whistle was blown and the guard waved his flag, the train sped off into the countryside. After about half an hour, it stopped at the village of Howden, about 20 miles from Hull. All of the children and Leena clambered out of the carriages and stood on the station platform where they were inspected by a group of middle-class ladies from the local Women's Institute. Molly noticed that they were all wearing what was colloquially termed by the children as 'piss-pot' hats.

Some of the evacuees were quickly selected, and the platform soon began to empty. As Leena stood there with Molly, no one seemed interested in taking a middle-aged woman and her child. But eventually, a lady from the Woman's Institute managed to persuade a Mrs. Nutbrown to take them and they all trooped off together to her house down Bridgegate, where the woman lived with her policeman husband.

The next day Molly was enrolled at the village school, but soon had to change her classes and join a higher form as her learning was well above that of her year group.

While Molly attended school, Leena found work 'tati scratting', gathering potatoes on a local farm. Her job was to pick up the potatoes which had been turned up by a tractor as it moved slowly along in front of her and the other farm workers. It was hard, backbreaking work, bending down to pick up and then place the earthy potatoes into a bucket. When the bucker was full, it had to be emptied them into a nearby trailer. The routine then started all over again. Leena, wearing her trusty washhouse wellingtons, followed the tractor until a field was cleared and would then start on the next one. At the end of a day's grafting, she was lucky to come away with just a few shillings.

Despite Mr. Nutbrown being the village policeman, when Leena departed at dawn for her farm work, Molly felt strange and didn't like being left in the house alone. So, after Leena had gone, she took to running down to the bottom of the rear garden to sit in the shed which housed the Nutbrown's only sanitation, an earth closet toilet. The toilet was filled with dry earth to absorb the urine and waste. It had two round holes with seats, placed side by side. When one hole appeared to be full, it was time to use the other. The earth toilet was emptied by a drawer being pulled out at the bottom of the seating. Once a week, the drawer and its contents were carried out and emptied by the 'Muck Cart' man into the back of his horse-drawn cart. Just like back at home in Bean Street, toilet paper consisted of old newspapers cut up into squares and dangling from a string.

One morning, Mr. Nutbrown, needing to relieve himself before setting off to work, visited the toilet. Finding the door locked, he had caught Molly in there. Waiting patiently outside for several minutes, he eventually shouted through the door asking Molly why she was taking so long. But Molly refused to come out and it took some time for Mr. Nutbrown to persuade her to open the door.

Shortly after this incident, Mr. Nutbrown asked Molly whether she could cook. When she said that she could, Mr. Nutbrown directed her to the kitchen where every morning she was given the task of cooking the breakfast porridge. Not only did it keep Molly out of the toilet, but Mr. Nutbrown now enjoyed his porridge as it had apparently been something which his wife had a tendency to burn.

Molly was popular at Howden School. There was no Miss Treff to deal with, and being keen and bright during her lessons there was a genuine liking for by the school's teachers. Molly also joined a local dancing school and appeared in a show.

One day, when Molly returned home from school, she heard her mother's voice desperately calling to her. Going through to the rear of the cottage, Molly found her mother firmly wedged in the dolly tub. She had been taking a bath and the hot water must have swollen her flesh. Because of the sloping shape of the tub, and the narrowness of its rim, she was unable to climb out. Leena was desperate and crying as she feared that Mr. Nutbrown might catch her in there. Molly, couldn't stop laughing, but eventually was able to help to pull her mother out.

After being in Howden for six months, Leena one day had a row with Mrs. Nutbrown. It was about how few clothes Molly had, and how most of them were ragged. The bombing had also eased back in Hull. So, Leena decided that they should both return home. The teachers at Howden School were sad to hear this and the Head Teacher offered to let Molly stay with her, but she couldn't accommodate Leena. Molly, despite enjoying her life in Howden, didn't want to stay there on her own and she was also missing her father. So, they eventually returned to the bomb scarred streets of Hull.

Just before they left, a cottage came up for rent came in Howden. and on their return home, Molly tried to persuade her father to go and take a look at it with a view to moving there. She explained to him about the different life they could live there, and how Fred would have his own garden. But Fred refused to move.

The Ashes, Howden

Chapter 9

Street Life

While Molly had been away, Selena's mother had, had another child, whom she'd christened Harold. It meant that Selena now had to spend more time indoors looking after him. A new girl had recently moved to Bean Street from Scarborough. Her father was a fisherman. The girl had latterly joined Molly's class at school. Her name was Annie Jowsey. As Selena couldn't come out much, Molly and Annie began to hang about together, playing on 'Regie swings' and roaming about the bombed streets of the area The two of them would often climb up onto a bombed-out bakehouse roof which was just around the corner from Poplar Terrace. Here with other children, they would hang from the derelict rafters. They would also on an evening gather outside Mrs. Gormley's sweetshop. On one occasion, when they were there, a Bean Street boy named Charlie Poulton joined them. He had a few days earlier appeared before the Hull Juvenile Court for stealing a bottle of lemonade from a horse drawn cart while the driver was doing his rounds. For his crime, he had received six strokes of the birch. This had involved him being tied to a tilted, wooden structure with arms spread out while a rod of birch twigs was applied to his buttocks. He had shown everyone, who wanted to see them, the marks, and even days later he still winced if anyone jostled him.

There was another sweet shop around the corner of Bean Street on Anlaby Road which Molly would regularly visit. The shop had boxes of sweets in the window and glass jars on its shelves. When some of the boiled sweet jars got down close to the bottom and there was only sugar waste left, the shopkeeper would pour all of the remaining waste into one jar. The contents of this jar could be bought cheaply. Molly would often buy some. The sweet waste would be poured into a small cone shaped paper bag. Holding the bag Molly would squeeze and compress it, breaking up the larger pieces of sweet so that they too became solid sugar dust. After finishing the manipulation, a tiny piece of the pointed part of the cone shaped bag would be torn off. Then holding the upturned bag tightly shut the cone would be applied to the mouth.

Molly attended Miss Neville's dancing school on the corner of Linneaus Street and in one production played a tipple-tailing golliwog. She also began attending music lessons, but having no piano, would pay a local girl sixpence to practice on hers. Molly would get the hard-earned money from her father. Turning up at the girl's house, after paying her fees, she would just get started going through her practice pieces when the girl would abruptly close the lid of the piano,

"My father's coming home," she'd say, you'll have to go!"

After the second time this happened, Molly declined the girl's kind offers to let her practice on her piano. The girl, beginning to miss the funding the instrument was bringing in, tried blackmailing her.

"If you don't come to my house to practice, I'll tell the teacher that you don't have a piano!" But Molly defied her threats.

Telling her mother of her plight, Leena, began making weekly payments on a rosewood piano that was for sale in a Hessle Road music shop. The piano cost £12, and until the final payment was made, the shop owner said that it wouldn't be delivered. Leena kept on paying five shillings every week and as the final payments neared, the shop kindly allowed for the piano to be delivered early.

The instrument was relatively ancient and had carved flowers on its legs. The ivory keys had also turned yellow, and the front of the keys had no ivory covering them, and were just bare wood. Nevertheless, Molly was proud of the instrument and could now run through her repertoire.

Molly had been given a adventure book which she treasured. It was full of colourful pictures and exciting stories. One day, a girl she brought home from her school was shown the book and begged to borrow it. Molly was reluctant, this was one of her most treasured possessions and she didn't really want to lend it. But being kindhearted and the girl promising to look after it, she eventually gave way.

Several days later, when Molly requested the book back, the girl procrastinated about it and said that she hadn't finished reading it yet. After two or three more days had gone by, Molly turned up at the girl's house and demanded the book back. The girl claimed that her younger brother had got hold of it and pulled it to bits. Molly requested to see the bits and the girl brought them to her. What had once been a gloriously illustrated book, full of richly coloured pictures and exciting stories, now consisted of just one side of the cardboard cover and a few ripped pages.

Selina was very good at getting to hear about forthcoming Christmas parties at some of the local churches and youth clubs. She would tell Molly and as it neared Xmas the two of them would join these organisations for the short-term. They enlisted in such groups as the Girls Training Co, the Salvation Army and the Girls Brigade. Being a member meant that they would be able to attend their parties and receive a gift at Xmas.

Molly and Selena would also go to the local cinemas, including the Langham on Hessle Road, the West Park Palace on Anlaby Road, Princes Hall down George Street and the Playhouse on Porter Street.

The Playhouse ran a children's film show on a Saturday and local children would queue up outside to see it. Once the doors opened, a commissioner would attempt to hold back the thronging crowd of children, while the usherette attempted to collect their one penny entrance fees. The sheer weight of the kids, with those without money pushing at the back, meant that many would get in for free. When she was younger, Molly had once visited the cinema for the children's matinee on her own and when she had returned home, told her mother that while she was there the man playing the organ had winked at her. Leena had got her coat on and marched down to the cinema to remonstrate with the management. The cinema staff were baffled as the cinema never had an organ. Then they suddenly realised that the man had featured in one of the on-screen films.

One winter, when the snow had lain frozen on the ground for several weeks, Molly made a snowball and threw it at the back of the neck of a man driving a horse and cart. The man immediately left his horse and cart behind and chased Molly down the length of Bean Street. Just when she was out of breath and about to give up, the man thankfully stopped chasing her, but he shook a fist and said, "I'll get you, you bastard." Because of her distinctive auburn hair, he soon found out where she lived and when no one answered the door of 12 Poplar terrace, he punched in one of the door panels.

Even though Fred had returned from his internment, Leena had continued working as a domestic. She would often be out all-day cleaning to earn a few shillings. Fred would every evening wash Molly's socks, and warm her scarf and gloves on the Belgium stove ready for school the next day.

Molly's dog Rover had continued to only respond to her and if anyone else came near him he would growl at them, warning them off. One day he was waiting on the step of 12 Poplar Terrace to be let in and a young child from around the corner of the terrace, stroked him and he bit her. The child's parents complained to the police and Fred had to attend Hull Magistrate's court. Molly went along with him and as Fred stood before the magistrate, speaking in his broken English it was proving difficult for the court to understand him and Molly had to speak on his behalf. Nevertheless, the judge still directed that Rover be put down. But when he saw Molly in floods of tears, he relented and ordered that Rover should in future not be allowed out without a muzzle.

The complainants lived just around the corner of the terrace and for months a thumping sound had been heard coming from their house, like the sound of a printing press. A few months later the man of the house appeared in court for printing counterfeit tickets for Hull City's football matches.

Hessle Road Woolworth

Princes Hall, George Street

Parliament Street

Chapter 10

LEAVING SCHOOL

Leena had received a letter explaining that Molly would benefit by going onto Grammar School., but this meant buying a uniform, which would have been impossible.

Despite being the school captain, the swimming captain and the Red House captain, Molly couldn't wait to leave school. She enjoyed studying and all of her lessons, but her time at school was spoilt by Miss Treff. She had developed a strong disliking for her and leaving school meant escaping her. She didn't pick on most of the other girls in the class, like Gertie Smith, who would often sit with the desk lid up having a fag.

A couple of weeks before Molly was due to leave school. Miss Treff picked on her for the last time.

"Wipe that smile off your face, or, I'll knock it off." She told Molly.

But Molly had, had enough and plucking up her courage she pushed back her desk and told Miss. Treff in no uncertain terms, "If you hit me, I'll hit you back!" Miss Treff was stunned by Molly's retaliation and simply walked away. She never spoke to Molly again before she left school.

Gertie Smith and Annie Woodward had their names down for the woodyard. Annie was going to back a saw. But Fred had told Molly in his broken English. "You don't want to be getting covered in muck and wearing a turban, get yourself a job in an office!" He had seen the office staff at Atkinson and Prickett, seemingly sitting around on their backsides doing absolutely nothing.

When the school bell had rung for that last time, Molly had run all the way home, expecting at any minute to be dragged back by Miss. Treff or told that she would have to stay on for another year.

When the reality finally set in that she was free and would never have to attend school again Molly began to apply for jobs advertised in the Hull Daily Mail. The first job she applied for was as an office junior with the company of W.N. Lewendon and Sons, a firm of auctioneers and valuers, based at 4 Parliament Street, Hull. Their office was situated almost opposite Hull's old Police Station. Molly discovered that the middleclass staff at Lewendon's spoke with plums in their mouths. She attended her interview wearing her school clothes, as those were the best she had. Both Molly and another girl were taken on. The other girl, Peggy, came up every day from Hornsea on the train. Like the rest of the staff, she was also from a middle-class background, but she and Molly got on well together. Peggy showed little reverence for her peers and would address the rest of the staff as her equals. "Hunt, Hunt!" she would exclaim when the senior clerk was required on the telephone. "It's Mr. Hunt to you!" she would be reminded by the office manager.

The office manager, a middle-aged lady, was also responsible for acting as secretary to each of Lewendon's partners. When they required a letter writing, a bell would ring and she would disappear off into one of the partner's office's and take the letter down a letter in shorthand before later having it typed up. One day she was late back from lunch and the bell went, so Molly took up a pad and a pencil and went into the partner's office. She sat down in a chair next to the partner's desk ready to take down the notes. Looking up the partner was surprised to see her sitting there, and when she explained that the Office Manager was out, he asked her if she felt capable of taking down the letter. She said she was, as she had learnt shorthand at night school. He then duly dictated the letter to her and later she typed it out.

Peggy and Molly's employment included working Saturday mornings. One weekend, when there were there and there were few staff around, they decided to explore the labyrinth of passages in the basement beneath the offices of 4 Parliament Street. They discovered a small room which had a wall mirror in it and they sat there doing their hair and makeup. Suddenly, they could hear footsteps down the steps into the basement and then the huge figure of Colonel Lewendon blocked the doorway. They had never seen him before as he had just returned from the war. "Who are you?" he demanded brusquely of the pair of them. When they told him, his demeanor changed for the better, and he simply said, "You shouldn't be down here, go back to your offices".

Whitefriargate

After work on a Saturday morning, Peggy and Molly would go shopping around town. Peggy was allowed to keep the whole of her wages, and they visited most of the shops down Whitefriargate. When Molly had received her first wage packet and taken it home, Leena was hoping for some 'board money', a contribution to the household expenditure. But Molly had seen a dress that she desperately needed for work and they ended up spending more than she had earned in wages.

After a few months of working at Lewendons', one Friday evening Molly brought her wage packet home, and after opening it, discovered that that there was a pound more than what she was usually paid. Optimistic, she thought that it might have been given it for doing good work. But her father urged her to return it as he thought that it might be a test of her honesty. On the Monday morning she returned the extra pound to the Office Manager and nothing more was said of it. But a week later the firm decided that it only needed one office junior and Peggy was asked to leave.

That year, Leena, Molly and Fred went to Hull Fair where they bought a ticket for Chicken Joe's prize stall. Lights flashed on the sequence of numbers allocated to each of the players and eventually the light stopped on the one that Molly chosen. Chicken Joe told the crowd that she had won a ham, a chicken, a bag of groceries and any prize off the stall. "Don't forget your custard, he had said as he'd handed her the groceries." Molly chose a tea set as her main prize, and with the shortage of such items in wartime Britain, Chicken Joe tried to buy back off her for three pounds. But Molly hung onto it. On the way home, walking down a pitch-black Bean Street, a man suddenly came out of the darkness of one of the bombed building sites and Leena called him all the names under the sun for startling them.

On 17 July 1944, Leena, who had since 1929 been classed as a German, gained her Naturalisation Certificate and was readmitted as a British citizen.

The Cooperative Store on Jameson Street

Whitefriargate

Paragon Street

Grandma Land

Chapter 11
Seaside

For many years, Leena had been banned from visiting her parent's home due to her marrying a German, so Molly had never met her grandparents. But around the age of nine, Leena had been out with Molly down town and they had met her mother. After some initial awkwardness, it was arranged that Leena should bring Molly to see her in her house down Jennings Street, off Cleveland Street and later, when her home was bombed, to her house down Alaska Street. These meetings had to be clandestine and take place when Leena's father was out at work on the railways.

Molly liked the Jennings Street house, which had a huge bay window. During her visits, she would offer to do odd jobs for her grandma, such as polishing the bath's brass taps. But grandma Land would usually say that all of the jobs had already been done by her adopted daughter, Nelly. During these visits, while at the house, Molly would also often meet two of her mother's sisters. Her kind auntie Doris, and her much sterner auntie Ethel. From then on there was also always a present to be had from her grandma at Xmas, especially dollies.

Mrs. Land had four daughters, but one of them, Minnie, had become pregnant on one of her future husband's returns from the battlefields during the first world war. The child, Nelly, had been born with consumption and wasn't expected to live long. So, Mrs. Land had taken her on and brought her up as her own. Nelly survived childhood and when you got older, she took over the running of Grandma Land's house carrying out all of the domestic chores.

Sadly, when she was only in her twenties, Nelly died, and a few months later Mrs. Land's husband also died. His body was laid resting in the front room of their Alaska Street home.

On the day of the funeral, Molly and Leena turned up at the house ready for the trip to Hull's Eastern Cemetery. The house was crowded as the family waited for the cortege to arrive to carry their husband and father off. On arrival Leena had immediately gone to console her mother, whilst Molly went to hang her coat up in the front room as she always did.

Turning around after hanging up her coat, she was greeted by the sight of the open coffin with her grandfather's face staring up at her. It had been a hot summer and Mr. Land had been laid there for a week, and his body was slowly starting to decompose. His features now had a tinge of green to them, due to the decomposition. On seeing it, a scream went up from Molly, which immediately brought the rest of the household to the room, and she was led away in tears.

For weeks afterwards, Molly would wake up on a night screaming, seeing her grandfather's face in her dream.

Leena discussed this with her mother, and because of the trauma that Molly had suffered. Mrs. Land suggested that she, Leena and Molly should enjoy a week's holiday at Scarborough.

On the day the holiday was due to start Fred carried the suitcases as he accompanied Leena and Molly down to Paragon Station. Here for the first time, he met Leena's mother, Mrs. Land. After an awkward beginning, Fred contributed to the conversation in his broken English and within minutes Mrs. Land realized that her daughter had married a decent man.

After arriving off the train in Scarborough, rooms were found at a boarding house off Westborough on Bland's Cliff. The landlady there obligingly offered to cook any food her guests brough to her. So for their tea Leena and Granny Land brought her fish to cook.

The next day Molly enjoyed visiting Scarborough's open-air, sea water filled, swimming pool. The next day she joined a party of other holiday makers and took a rowing boat trip out of the harbour. She soon regretted it when the sea became choppy and a fish landed on the end of her oar.

On an evening entertainment was had at the Spa, where a virtuoso at the organ made the audience feel virtually seasick when he played them his own composition, 'Storm at Sea'.

Every day the three of them would stroll the promenade and pass by the many amusement arcades along the seafront. On a visit to one, Molly spotted a large glass-cased machine which featured a shipwreck and pirate treasure spread-out on a rock-strewn bottom of the sea. The machine claimed that it gave out a prize every time.

Molly place a coin into the payment slot, and the small figure of an underwater diver, wearing a diving helmet, walked along the bottom of the seabed to collect her a gift. The gifts came in small white boxes. Molly watched intently as the diver collected her prize. He then walked with it towards the hold of the sunken ship, to which was attached the chute down which the gifts came out. But as the diver holding the small boxed gift made his way towards her, Molly stared at the face in the diving helmet. It was coloured a garish green and instantly reminded her of the face of her dead grandfather. Letting out a continuous scream she was soon surrounded by passersby who wondered what the trouble was. Then Leena and her grandmother took her out of the place. The green face of the diver had brought back the shock of seeing her decomposing grandfather.

There were further visits to Scarborough by the three of them, but eventually Leena's occasional difficultness on one trip upset Grandma Land and she went home early. After that the visits ceased.

Botanic Gardens Railway Station

Stepney Station

Chapter 11

Night school

Soon after leaving school and starting work, Molly began attending evening classes at the Boulevard night-school. This was to develop her typewriting and shorthand skills. There she met a different crowd of people, and it would lead to Sunday bike rides to Hornsea, attending ballroom classes down Baker Street, and weekly dances at Dance Deluxe on Anlaby Road.

Fred had continued his job as the fire watchman at Atkinson and Prickett down the Land of Green Ginger and he would be away all-night returning home the following morning. Leena too, began to be absent for most of the evening. After completing her daytime cleaning duties at a private house, to earn a few extra shillings, on an evening, she began acting as a maid for the household, serving tea and waiting on the guests at an evening card game. This meant that she would often not get home until after 10 pm at night most evenings.

Molly would have to leave night school and pedal her bike all the way along a totally blacked out Anlaby Road, before cycling down an even darker Bean Street. The street was also blacked-out, with only the white fluorescent paint on the bottom of lampposts helping to show her the way.

Passing the recently bombed remains of derelict houses, and the eerie flapping of a parachute from a landmine hanging in the trees, Molly was half out of her wits. On reaching Poplar Terrace, she'd throw her bicycle up again the open entrance of the air raid shelter. Then turning her back on it, in the pitch-black she would try to get her key into the lock on the front door. Even when she managed to get the door open, she'd have to enter a pitch-black house before being able to put a light on. Then she would sit in the empty house with the sound of rats scuttling in the roof of the tiny kitchen. Sometime after ten o'clock she'd hear a faint sound in the passageway leading to the front door.

"Is that you mother?" she'd shout, but often there'd be no reply. Then eventually the front door would open and Leena would come in. "Is that you, mother?" Molly would repeat, and a voice would eventually say, "Who the do you think it is!"

Molly begged her mother not to do her night shift, but Leena would say, 'We need the money."

Some nights Molly would get Malcolm, one of the crowd from her evening classes, to follow her home. But sometimes he couldn't and anyway Molly thought that the way he shot off on his bike down a blacked-out Bean Street after dropping her off at Poplar Terrace, he seemed almost as frightened as her.

Eventually, the stress of having to cycle home in the pitch black and stand in a terrace, down which most of the houses were either bombed or unoccupied, with her back to an empty air raid shelter, became too much for her, and she stopped attending night school altogether.

Dancing at Dance Deluxe, Anlaby Road, Hull

The Tivoli stage backcloth, as you waited for the show to start

The Broadway Hotel

Chapter 12

The Broadway Hotel

When Peggy left Lewendons, the place didn't seem the same and Molly began to look around for another job. When she handed in her notice, and her employers had asked her why she wanted to leave. She had naively, quoted Leena, "My mother says the job's not worth the shoe leather!" She was referring to her three pounds wages. Nevertheless, several weeks after her departing, when Colonel Lewendon met Molly down Whitefriargate, he had urged her to return.

After leaving, Molly had considered joining the women's branch of one of the armed services, but Leena must have read the interview letter and followed her to the recruitment office. She then applied for a telephonist's position with the GPO down Lowgate. When she turned up for the interview several other girls were there filling in application forms, one of the girls was Joan Taylor from her old school. On see Molly, Joan immediately stood up and shouted to the rest of the girls, "It's no good us bothering, she's bound to get the job!"

As it happened, Molly decided not to continue with her application as she had also applied for a vacancy as receptionist at the Broadway Hotel, down Ferensway in the city centre. A popular hotel, it attracted both businessmen and passing entertainers. Many of the acts performing at one of Hull's many music halls would stay there.

When Molly turned up at the hotel, she was interviewed by the manager, Miss McBean. A middle-aged Scottish lady, Miss. McBean was known by her staff as 'Madam'.

Madam was a genteel lady in her sixties who spoke in a brogue Scottish. She had an apartment on the first floor of the hotel which was decorated in keeping with her Victorian upbringing.

When Molly told Madam how much she had been earning at Lewendon's, she told her that she couldn't possibly pay her that amount to someone so young, but to subsidise her wages she would get a meal at work every day.

Despite the job paying less per week, Molly accepted Madam's offer of employment and became the Broadway hotel's receptionist, sitting at a desk at a window overlooking Ferensway.

For Molly, working at the Broadway Hotel was like entering another world. Every day was different. Several members of the staff slept in and the housemaids had rooms in in roof attics.

When Big Bill Campbell, a popular Country and Western entertainer and radio star from Canada came to stay at the hotel, he brought with him his band, the Rocky Mountain Rhythm group. The outfit were appearing at the Tivoli Theatre down Paragon Street. When Big Bill departed, he left behind a full chamber pot under his bed, which had to be emptied by Hilda, the chamber maid, who was responsible for the rooms on the first floor. Hilda was quick to inform the rest of the hotel staff how she now knew how Big Bill had got his name.

Part of Molly's job was to once a week count the provisions in the hotel's store store. The war was still on and on opening the store cupboard door she was greeted by an abundance of edible riches. Because of rationing and the temptation that she might be faced with, Madam agreed to provide Molly with a small parcel of food each week, this always included a thin sliver of blue Stilton cheese which Molly's father Fred was much appreciated.

Once day while she was counting the stores. Molly ate a small fragment of cheese. On hearing voices, she turned round was much perturbed to discover an American football team, who were staying at the hotel, lining the stairs behind her. "We saw you!" they all shouted.

The Broadway was owned by local Brewers Moors and Robson and every year they held a soiree at the Beverley Road Baths for their employees. Molly loved dancing and went to the venue with her work colleagues who she had made friends with at the hotel. As she danced, she was surprised to find that she kept being picked out in the spotlight and won several spot prizes. She discovered later that it was a man from the Broadway who had purposely been shining the beam of light on her.

Chapter 13

Victory

As the war came to an end, to mark the cessation, the ringing of church bells rang out throughout Hull and the city centre was decorated in bunting and decorative lights. Formal events to mark the end of the war included a victory parade and a service of thanksgiving held at Holy Trinity Church. To celebrate the armistice, open air dances were also arranged in many of Hull parks, including West Park, East Park, Pearson's Park and Queen's Gardens. Military bands played at each of these events.

The dates of May 7, 8 and 9 may were days of celebration. Down the terraces of Bean Street and beyond, victory signs were painted on air raid shelters and terrace walls. Free Union Jack flags were distributed to the children of Hull. Speeches were delivered by dignitaries at Queens Gardens and thousands of people attended on the grass. The Lord Mayor spoke of the bombing campaigns, the loss of life and the bravery of all those in the city throughout the war, including first aiders, fire wardens, messengers, police, doctors, nurses, the National Fire Service and the citizens themselves.

Bonfires, which had been illegal during the war, were lit by children in the backstreets of Hull, and Hessle Road was alive with flag waving residents. Tea parties were arranged for the children down most of the residential streets and terraces across the city. Just like in London, people danced in the Queens Gardens fountains.

The celebrations culminated with a procession of thousands of children wearing fancy dress parading down Ferensway. The following day there was a parade of the armed forces and all of the other services who had played their part during the war. These included air raid wardens, WRACs, WRENS, Home Guards, ARP Wardens, Civil Defence volunteers, Land Army girls, nurses, factory workers, telephone workers, etc. Everybody who had done their bit.

The long possession assembled down the bottom of Alfred Gelder Street and marched past Ferens Art Gallery, where the Lord Mayor, the Sherriff of Hull and numerous other leading lights of the city took the salute.

Victoria Square was a mass of cheering crowds as literally, thousands of troops and organisations marched past, continuing on down Carr Lane and Ferensway.

As the war came to an end, the world and the city of Hull had been changed forever, after it lives would never be the same again.

A Devastated Queen Victoria Square on VE Day

The Victory Parades, May 1945, down Carr Lane and Ferensway

Dereliction, Bean Street in the 1960s, the final days

Air Raid Casualties

Bean Street

Marsay, Mary Thornton - 62 yrs - 15 Mar 1941 - 3 De la Pole Terr, Hull, ERY

Marshall, Dora - 62 yrs - 15 Mar 1941 - 10 De la Pole Terr, Hull, ERY

Moore, Donald - 3 yrs - 15 Mar 1941 - 6 De la Pole Terr, Bean St, Hull, ERY

Moore, Edith - 30 yrs - 15 Mar 1941 - 6 De la Pole Terr, Bean St, Hull, ERY

Moore, Frederick - 38 yrs - 15 Mar 1941 - 6 De la Pole Terr, Bean St, Hull, ERY

Moore, George - 6 yrs - 15 Mar 1941 - 6 De la Pole Terr, Bean St, Hull, ERY

Black, Louis (ARW,FW) - 49 yrs - 8 May 1941 - 78 Regent St, Hull, ERY

Garside, Florence Ida - 45 yrs - 15 Mar 1941 - De la Pole Terr, Hull, ERY

Garside, Thomas - 53 yrs - 15 Mar 1941 - De la Pole Terr, Hull, ERY

Robinson, Bertie - 65 yrs - 15 Mar 1941 - 11 De la Pole Terr, Bean St, Hull, ERY

Norris, Annie - 45 yrs - 15 Mar 1941 - 2 De la Pole Terr, Bean St, Hull, ERY

Norris, Marion - 8 yrs - 15 Mar 1941 - 2 De la Pole Terr, Bean St, Hull, ERY

Shaw, Lilian - 52 yrs - 15 Mar 1941 - De la Pole Terr, Bean St, Hull, ERY

Stockdale, Alice - 70 yrs - 15 Mar 1941 - 1 De la Pole Terr, Bean St, Hull, ERY

Stockdale, George - 74 yrs - 15 Mar 1941 - 1 De la Pole Terr, Bean St, Hull, ERY

Regent Street

Greenley, Amy Gibson - 27 yrs - 8 May 1941 - Regent St Shelter, Hull, ERY

Greenley, William - 23 mos - 8 May 1941 - Regent St Shelter, Hull, ERY

Borrill, Jane Isabella (WVS) - 58 yrs - 8 May 1941 - Regent St Shelter, Hull, ERY

Greenley, William James - 57 yrs - 8 May 1941 - Regent St Shelter, Hull, ERY

Lister, Bessie - 27 yrs - 8 May 1941 - Regent St Shelter, Hull, ERY

Lister, Robert William - 5 yrs - 8 May 1941 - Regent St Shelter, Hull, ERY

Moody, Dorothea Mary - 7 yrs - 8 May 1941 - La Trobe Terr, Regent St, Hull, ERY

Moody, Mary Elizabeth - 60 yrs - 8 May 1941 - La Trobe Terr, Regent St, Hull, ERY

O'Brian, Doreen - 13 yrs - 8 May 1941 - La Trobe Terr, Regent St, Hull, ERY

O'Brian, Florrie - 43 yrs - 8 May 1941 - 8 La Trobe Terr, Regent St, Hull, ERY

O'Brian, Thomas - 45 yrs - 8 May 1941 - 8 La Trobe Terr, Regent St, Hull, ERY

Richardson, Gerald - 13 yrs - 8 May 1941 - La Trobe Terr, Regent St, Hull

Smith, Walter - 58 yrs - 8 May 1941 - La Trobe Terr, Hull,

Taylor, Florence - 55 yrs - 8 May 1941 - La Trobe Terr, Regent St, Hull, ERY

Trushell, Florence - 18 yrs - 8 May 1941 - La Trobe Terr, Regent St, Hull, ERY

Carter, Brenda - 18 mos - 8 May 1941 - La Trobe Terr Shelter, Hull, ERY

Carter, Olive May - 27 yrs - 8 May 1941 - La Trobe Terr Shelter, Hull, ERY

Carter, William George - 35 yrs - 8 May 1941 - La Trobe Terr Shelter, Hull, ERY

Frederick Raigrotzki

Epithet: Knockaloe Camp internee, Isle of Man

Record type: First World War Internees

Biography: Released from Knockaloe 10.9.1919.
Ref. 264/1772. Prisoner of War Information Bureau serial
number: 2551. (MS 09395 Koblenz ref R67/1756-1772
page 43.)

Gender: Male

Naturisation Certificate: **Eleanor Raigrotzki**.

From Germany. Resident in Hull.

Certificate DZ2745 issued 17 July 1944…..

Home Office: Immigration and Nationality Department: Duplicate
Certificates of Naturalisation, Declarations of British Nationality,
and Declaration of Alienage. 1914 British Nationality and Status of
Aliens.

Naturalisation Certificate: Eleanor Raigrotzki. From Germany.
Resident in Hull. Certificate DZ2745 issues 17 July 1944.

Note(s): Readmission.

Fire Watcher (Business Premises)

Personnel card

Reference No:
C TYR/18/2/3232

Dates:
11 Dec 1942

Description:
Name: F. Raigrotzki

Age: 67

Home address: 12 Poplar Terrace, Bean Street, Hull

Employed by: Atkinson and Prickett Ltd

Firewatching at: Land of Green Ginger, Hull

Date: 11 Dec 1942

Hull Celebrates VE-Day

PREPARATIONS FOR BIG NIGHT OF REJOICING

HULL, one of Britain's hardest hit cities of the war, celebrated the end of European hostilities to-day in a quiet and restrained manner but with a profound feeling of thankfulness.